**Put Beginning Readers on the Right Track with
ALL ABOARD READING™**

The All Aboard Reading series is especially designed for beginning readers. Written by noted authors and illustrated in full color, these are books that children really want to read—books to excite their imagination, expand their interests, make them laugh, and support their feelings. With fiction and nonfiction stories that are high interest and curriculum-related, All Aboard Reading books offer something for every young reader. And with four different reading levels, the All Aboard Reading series lets you choose which books are most appropriate for your children and their growing abilities.

Picture Readers
Picture Readers have super-simple texts, with many nouns appearing as rebus pictures. At the end of each book are 24 flash cards—on one side is a rebus picture; on the other side is the written-out word.

Station Stop 1
Station Stop 1 books are best for children who have just begun to read. Simple words and big type make these early reading experiences more comfortable. Picture clues help children to figure out the words on the page. Lots of repetition throughout the text helps children to predict the next word or phrase—an essential step in developing word recognition.

Station Stop 2
Station Stop 2 books are written specifically for children who are reading with help. Short sentences make it easier for early readers to understand what they are reading. Simple plots and simple dialogue help children with reading comprehension.

Station Stop 3
Station Stop 3 books are perfect for children who are reading alone. With longer text and harder words, these books appeal to children who have mastered basic reading skills. More complex stories captivate children who are ready for more challenging books.

In addition to All Aboard Reading books, look for All Aboard Math Readers™ (fiction stories that teach math concepts children are learning in school); All Aboard Science Readers™ (nonfiction books that explore the most fascinating science topics in age-appropriate language); All Aboard Poetry Readers™ (funny, rhyming poems for readers of all levels); and All Aboard Mystery Readers™ (puzzling tales where children piece together evidence with the characters).

All Aboard for happy reading!

D1114111

For Captain Clara and the Dadoba—L.D.

To those who pursue research to understand
and save the life in the oceans—C.W.

GROSSET & DUNLAP
Published by the Penguin Group
Penguin Group (USA) Inc., 375 Hudson Street, New York, New York 10014, U.S.A.
Penguin Group (Canada), 90 Eglinton Avenue East, Suite 700, Toronto, Ontario,
Canada M4P 2Y3 (a division of Pearson Penguin Canada Inc.)
Penguin Books Ltd, 80 Strand, London WC2R 0RL, England
Penguin Ireland, 25 St Stephen's Green, Dublin 2, Ireland
(a division of Penguin Books Ltd)
Penguin Group (Australia), 250 Camberwell Road, Camberwell, Victoria 3124, Australia
(a division of Pearson Australia Group Pty Ltd)
Penguin Books India Pvt Ltd, 11 Community Centre, Panchsheel Park,
New Delhi - 110 017, India
Penguin Group (NZ), Cnr Airborne and Rosedale Roads, Albany, Auckland 1310, New Zealand
(a division of Pearson New Zealand Ltd)
Penguin Books (South Africa) (Pty) Ltd, 24 Sturdee Avenue, Rosebank,
Johannesburg 2196, South Africa

Penguin Books Ltd, Registered Offices:
80 Strand, London WC2R 0RL, England

Text copyright © 2006 by Laura Driscoll. Illustrations copyright © 2006 by Christina Wald.
All rights reserved. Published by Grosset & Dunlap, a division of Penguin Young Readers
Group, 345 Hudson Street, New York, New York 10014. ALL ABOARD SCIENCE READER
and GROSSET & DUNLAP are trademarks of Penguin Group (USA) Inc. Printed in the U.S.A.

Library of Congress Cataloging-in-Publication Data

Driscoll, Laura.
  Do dolphins really smile? / by Laura Driscoll ; illustrated by Christina Wald.
    p. cm. — (All aboard science reader. Station stop 2)
  ISBN 0-448-44341-4
  1. Dolphins—Psychology—Juvenile literature. 2. Learning in animals—Juvenile literature. 3.
Animal intelligence. I. Wald, Christina, ill. II. Title. III. Series.
  QL737.C432D75 2006
  599.53—dc22
                            2005027808

10 9 8 7 6 5 4 3 2 1

Do Dolphins Really Smile?

By Laura Driscoll
Illustrated by Christina Wald

Grosset & Dunlap

New York Aquarium
Brooklyn, New York
1998

Two dolphins play together
in a large pool.
Their names are Tab and Presley.

Tab chases Presley.

Presley dives down.

Tab dives after Presley.

Like all dolphins, they love to play!

5

They like to eat, too.

Now it is feeding time!

A trainer blows a whistle.

The dolphins race to her.

She tosses fish to them.

They catch the fish in their mouths.

Soon feeding time is over.

What is the trainer holding now?

Is it another fish?

No. It is a marker.

She makes a mark on Tab's head.

8

On the other side of the pool,

there is a mirror.

Right away Tab swims to it.

Tab floats in front of the mirror.

He looks at himself.

He tries to see the mark on his head.

Scientists are watching Tab.

Why are they there?

They want to know the answer
to a question.

Does Tab recognize himself?

It seems like he does.

He looks at the mark.

Tab seems to know it is Tab in the mirror—
not some other dolphin.

Besides dolphins,

only humans and apes

know their own images

in a mirror.

So dolphins must be very smart.

Just <u>how</u> smart are they?

Scientists don't know for sure.

But there is a lot

they <u>do</u> know about dolphins.

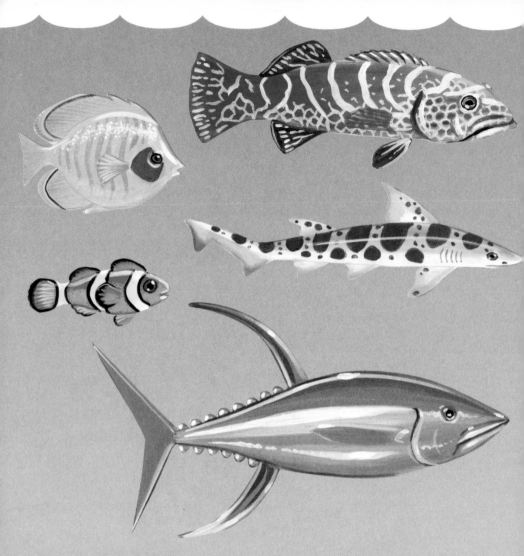

Do you know that dolphins are not fish?

Dolphins may look like fish.

But fish breathe underwater

through slits called gills.

Their babies hatch from eggs.

Dolphins are mammals,

like dogs and cows and humans.

They breathe air.

They give birth to live babies.

They nurse their young.

Dolphins are a kind of whale.

The biggest whales are

much bigger than dolphins.

But they all belong to the same family.

Blue whale (up to 100 feet)

Beluga whale (up to 19 feet)

Sperm whale (up to 70 feet)

Narwhal (up to 20 feet)

Humpback whale (up to 60 feet)

There are many different types
of dolphins.

Bottlenose dolphin

Spinner dolphin

Spotted dolphin

Common dolphin

Boto River dolphin

Baiji River dolphin

Dolphins live in many parts
of the world.

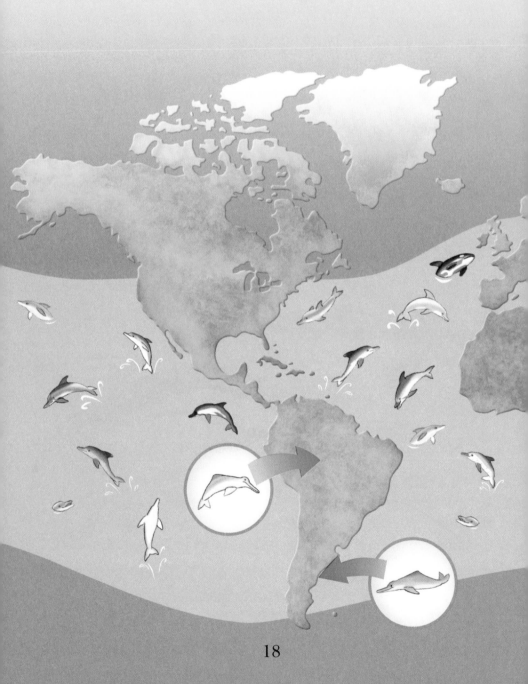

Some live in the ocean.

Some live in rivers.

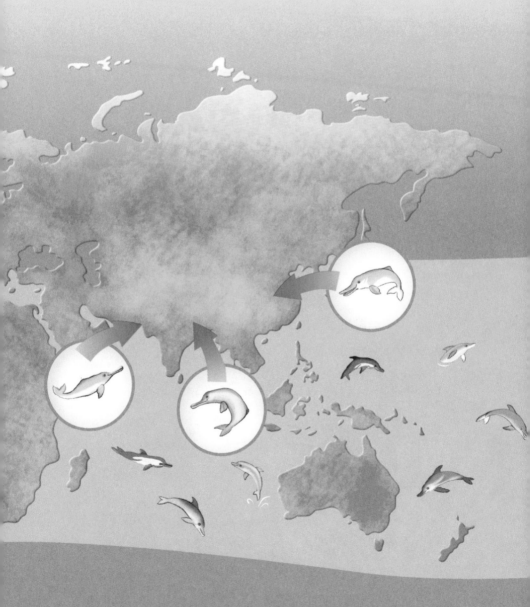

Most dolphins you see in aquariums
are bottlenose dolphins.
They have sleek bodies
and powerful tails.
They can swim 30 miles per hour!

These are the dolphins that look

like they are smiling.

But are they really? Scientists say no.

They look this way even

when they are scared.

Like all whales,

a dolphin must hold

its breath underwater.

Some dolphins can hold their

breath for ten minutes!

Then they come up for air.

There is a hole on top of a dolphin's head.

It is called a blowhole.

It opens to take in air.

Then the dolphin dives down

in the water again.

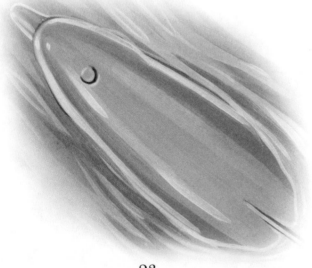

In the ocean, bottlenose dolphins

live in small groups.

Sometimes groups will band together.

There may be hundreds of dolphins.

They swim together.

They care for their young together.

They hunt for food together.

They form a circle

around a group of fish.

Some of the dolphins

swim into the circle and eat fish.

When they are done,

the next group of dolphins

gets a turn to eat.

How do dolphins work so well together?

Some scientists think

they "talk" to each other.

Lots of animals tell each other things.

Dogs growl to say, "Back off."

They whine to show

they are scared or hurt.

Their grunts are like

happy sighs.

And their barks can

mean many different things.

Dolphins also make different sounds.

They whistle.

They squeal.

They click—a sound like

a creaky door opening.

What do dolphins tell each other?

A scientist did an experiment to find out.

He used one light and two switches—

left and right.

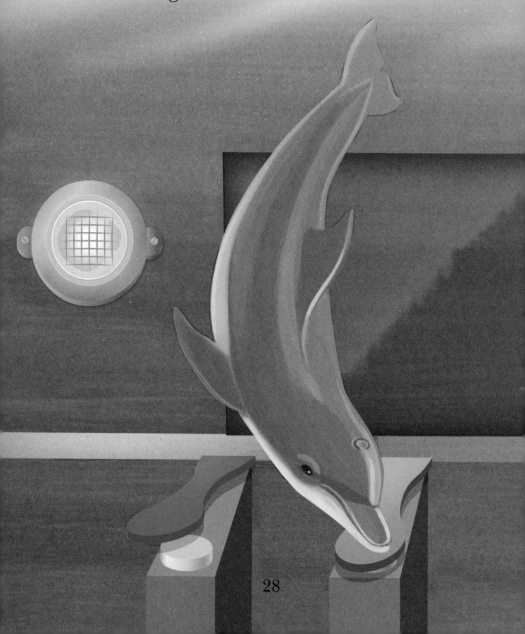

He worked with two dolphins.

Their names were Buzz and Doris.

Sometimes the light came on and stayed on.

That told the dolphins

to hit the switch on the right.

If they both did it,

they got a treat—a fish!

Then they were kept apart in the pool.

They could hear each other,

but they could not see each other.

Only Doris could see the light.

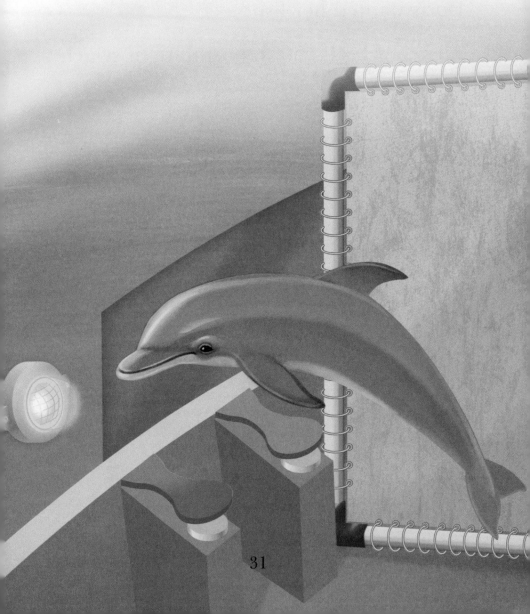

The light came on and stayed on.

Doris knew to hit the right switch.

But Buzz did not know

because he could not see the light.

Doris wanted her fish!

And they <u>both</u> had to hit the right switch

for her to get it.

She made a sound.

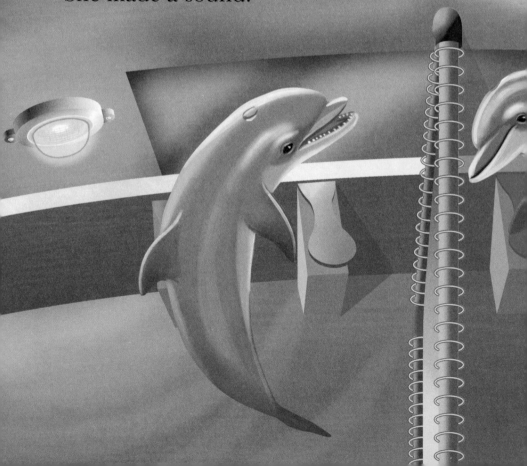

Buzz heard it.

Then he hit the right switch!

They both got their fish.

The scientist did the test

over and over.

Buzz knew the switch to hit

almost every time.

How did he know?

Did Doris tell him?

This dolphin looks for food in a coral reef.

She has a sponge on her snout.

Why did she put it there?

Because the coral is sharp.

She may be using the sponge

to protect her snout.

It is a smart thing for a dolphin to do.

Very smart.

These are the dolphin's babies.

They also put sponges on their snouts.

Did the mama dolphin teach them to?
Some scientists think so.

So dolphins may be good teachers.

They are definitely good students!

Dolphins in tanks

learn lots of tricks.

And they learn them quickly.

They stand on
their tail and dance
on the water.

They do flips in
the air.

They wave hello
with their flippers.

At one aquarium, bits of trash
sometimes got in the pool.
Eating trash can make
dolphins very sick.

So the trainers had an idea.
They trained the dolphins
to help clean the pool.

Each time the dolphins brought trash,

they got some fish.

The dolphins seemed to like this new game.

One dolphin came back
again,
and again,
and again.

Each time,

he had more trash.

Each time,

he got more fish.

But one thing didn't make sense.

The pool looked clean.

So where was the dolphin

finding all the trash?

The dolphin had

a secret stash of trash!

He had found lots of trash.

He had stuffed it all in a bag

in one corner of the pool.

Why did he do this?

To get fish!

When he wanted a snack,

he swam to the hidden trash.

He picked out a tiny piece,

or he tore off a small bit.

He wanted his stash to last.

Then he took the trash

to the trainer . . .

and got his fish!

The dolphin's new trick

was to trick the trainers!

So maybe dolphins don't smile.

But that one sure got the last laugh!